EMMANUEL JOSEPH

Culinary Code, The Fusion of Robotics, Sociology, and the Art of Eating

Contents

1

Chapter 1: The Dawn of Culinary Robotics

The fusion of culinary arts and robotics has revolutionized the way we approach food preparation. In the past, cooking was a manual process that relied heavily on human intuition and skill. However, with the advent of culinary robotics, machines now assist chefs in creating complex dishes with precision and consistency. These robots are equipped with advanced sensors and algorithms that allow them to measure ingredients, control temperatures, and execute intricate cooking techniques. This technological advancement has not only increased efficiency in professional kitchens but has also opened up new possibilities for home cooks.

The integration of robotics into the culinary world has also sparked a debate about the role of human creativity in cooking. While robots can replicate recipes with exact precision, they lack the ability to innovate and experiment in the same way that human chefs do. This has led to a renewed appreciation for the artistry and intuition that goes into creating a truly exceptional dish. As a result, many chefs are now embracing robotics as a tool to enhance their craft rather than replace it.

Moreover, the use of robotics in cooking has significant implications for food safety and hygiene. Robots can operate in controlled environments, reducing the risk of contamination and ensuring that food is prepared under optimal conditions. This is particularly important in large-scale food production, where maintaining consistent quality and safety standards is paramount. By minimizing human error and contamination, culinary robots contribute to a safer and more reliable food supply chain.

In addition to improving efficiency and safety, culinary robotics has the potential to make gourmet cooking more accessible to the general public. With user-friendly interfaces and step-by-step instructions, home cooks can now recreate restaurant-quality dishes in their own kitchens. This democratization of culinary expertise has inspired a new generation of food enthusiasts to explore and experiment with cooking, further blurring the lines between professional chefs and amateur cooks.

2

Chapter 2: The Sociology of Eating in the Age of Automation

The rise of culinary robotics has not only transformed the way we prepare food but also the way we consume and experience it. As automation becomes more prevalent in the kitchen, it is reshaping our social interactions and cultural practices around eating. Traditionally, meal preparation has been a communal activity that brings people together, fostering connections and shared experiences. However, the convenience and efficiency of robotic cooking challenge this notion, as individuals can now rely on machines to prepare meals independently.

This shift has prompted sociologists to examine the implications of automation on our eating habits and social dynamics. On one hand, the time saved through robotic cooking can be redirected towards other activities, such as spending quality time with loved ones or pursuing personal interests. On the other hand, the reliance on machines for meal preparation may lead to a decline in traditional cooking skills and a weakening of the cultural significance of shared meals.

Moreover, the integration of robotics into the culinary world raises questions about the future of food-related professions. As robots take over repetitive and labor-intensive tasks, the role of human chefs is evolving. While some fear that automation will lead to job displacement, others argue that it will create new opportunities for culinary innovation and specialization. Chefs can now focus on honing their creative skills, experimenting with new flavors and techniques, and pushing the boundaries of culinary artistry.

Furthermore, the sociology of eating in the age of automation extends to issues of access and equity. While culinary robotics has the potential to democratize gourmet cooking, it also highlights the digital divide between those who can afford and access advanced technology and those who cannot. Ensuring that the benefits of culinary automation are accessible to all is a critical consideration in addressing social and economic disparities.

The changing landscape of food preparation and consumption in the age of robotics is a reflection of broader societal trends towards automation and digitalization. As we continue to navigate these changes, it is essential to consider the social, cultural, and ethical implications of integrating robotics into our daily lives.

3

Chapter 3: The Art of Eating: A Sensory Experience

At the heart of the culinary world lies the art of eating—a sensory experience that engages all five senses and transcends mere sustenance. The rise of culinary robotics has added a new dimension to this experience, as machines can now assist in creating dishes that are not only delicious but also visually stunning and texturally intriguing. The precision and consistency offered by robotics enable chefs to experiment with intricate plating techniques, innovative textures, and novel flavor combinations, enhancing the overall sensory journey for diners.

The visual presentation of a dish plays a crucial role in the art of eating. With the help of robotics, chefs can achieve meticulous plating designs that would be challenging to execute by hand. Advanced robotic arms and tools allow for precise placement of ingredients, creating visually striking compositions that captivate diners before they even take their first bite. This attention to detail elevates the dining experience, transforming each meal into a work of art.

In addition to visual appeal, the texture of food is a key component of the sensory experience. Culinary robotics enables chefs to experiment with a wide range of textures, from silky smooth purees to crispy, delicate garnishes. By controlling cooking techniques with precision, robots can create textural contrasts that enhance the overall enjoyment of a dish. This level of control allows for innovative culinary creations that surprise and delight the palate.

Flavor is, of course, at the core of the art of eating. The use of robotics in the kitchen allows for precise measurement and control of ingredients, ensuring that flavors are balanced and harmonious. This precision enables chefs to experiment with bold and unconventional flavor pairings, pushing the boundaries of traditional cuisine. Additionally, robots can assist in the development of new cooking techniques, such as molecular gastronomy, which opens up a world of possibilities for flavor innovation.

Ultimately, the integration of robotics into the culinary world enhances the art of eating by providing chefs with the tools to create multi-sensory experiences that engage and delight diners. While the human touch remains essential in the creative process, the precision and consistency offered by robotics elevate the culinary arts to new heights, making each meal a feast for the senses.

4

Chapter 4: The Ethical Implications of Culinary Automation

The rise of culinary robotics brings with it a host of ethical considerations that must be addressed as we navigate this technological frontier. One of the primary concerns is the potential displacement of human workers in the food industry. As robots take on tasks traditionally performed by humans, there is a risk of job loss and economic disruption for those employed in food preparation and service. It is essential to consider the impact on workers and develop strategies to mitigate these effects, such as retraining programs and opportunities for new roles in the evolving culinary landscape.

Another ethical consideration is the issue of food equity and access. While culinary robotics has the potential to democratize gourmet cooking, it also highlights disparities in access to advanced technology. Ensuring that the benefits of automation are available to all, regardless of socio-economic status, is a critical challenge. This includes addressing the digital divide and ensuring that affordable and user-friendly robotic solutions are accessible to a wide range of communities.

The use of robotics in food production also raises questions about sustainability and environmental impact. Automation can lead to more efficient use of resources and reduce food waste by minimizing human error. However, the production and disposal of robotic equipment also have environmental implications. It is important to consider the lifecycle of these technologies and develop sustainable practices that minimize their ecological footprint.

Furthermore, the integration of robotics into the culinary world necessitates a discussion about the preservation of culinary traditions and cultural heritage. While robots can replicate recipes with precision, they lack the cultural context and historical knowledge that human chefs bring to their craft. It is crucial to balance the efficiency and innovation offered by robotics with the need to preserve and celebrate the rich culinary traditions that have been passed down through generations.

Addressing these ethical considerations requires a collaborative approach that involves chefs, technologists, policymakers, and the broader community. By engaging in open dialogue and developing thoughtful policies, we can ensure that the integration of robotics into the culinary world is guided by principles of equity, sustainability, and cultural preservation.

5

Chapter 5: Culinary Education and the Role of Robotics

The integration of robotics into the culinary world has significant implications for culinary education and training. As technology continues to advance, culinary schools and institutions are incorporating robotics into their curricula to prepare the next generation of chefs for the evolving landscape of food preparation. This includes teaching students how to operate and program robotic equipment, as well as understanding the principles of automation and its impact on the culinary arts.

One of the key benefits of incorporating robotics into culinary education is the ability to provide students with hands-on experience using advanced technology. This prepares them for careers in high-tech kitchens and enables them to stay competitive in a rapidly changing industry. By gaining proficiency with robotic tools, students can enhance their skills and expand their creative possibilities, opening up new avenues for culinary innovation.

In addition to technical training, culinary education must also emphasize the importance of creativity and intuition in cooking. While robots can assist with precise measurements and repetitive tasks, the human touch remains essential in the culinary arts. Teaching students to balance the use of technology with their own creative instincts ensures that they can leverage the benefits of robotics while preserving the artistry and innovation that define exceptional cuisine.

Furthermore, culinary education plays a crucial role in addressing the ethical and social implications of culinary robotics. By fostering a deeper understanding of the impact of automation on the food industry, students can develop a more nuanced perspective on the benefits and challenges of integrating technology into their craft. This includes discussions about job displacement, food equity, and cultural preservation, equipping future chefs with the knowledge and skills to navigate these complex issues.

Ultimately, the role of robotics in culinary education is to complement and enhance traditional training methods. By integrating technology into the curriculum, culinary schools can provide students with a comprehensive education that prepares them for the future of food preparation. This ensures that the next generation of chefs is equipped to embrace the possibilities of culinary robotics while preserving the rich traditions and artistry that define the culinary arts.

The rise of culinary robotics has paved the way for the development of fully automated restaurants, where robots handle everything from cooking to serving food. These robotic restaurants offer a glimpse into the future of dining, where technology and innovation transform the traditional dining experience. In these establishments, robots can prepare dishes with precision, ensuring consistent quality and presentation. Additionally, automated systems can streamline the ordering process, allowing customers to place orders through digital interfaces and receive their meals promptly.

One of the key benefits of robotic restaurants is the potential for increased efficiency and reduced wait times. By automating various aspects of the dining experience, these establishments can serve more customers in a shorter amount of time, enhancing overall satisfaction. Furthermore, the use of robotics can help reduce labor costs, making it possible for restaurants to offer high-quality meals at more affordable prices. This accessibility can democratize fine dining, allowing a wider range of people to enjoy gourmet cuisine.

The introduction of robotic restaurants also opens up new possibilities for personalized dining experiences. With advanced data analytics and machine learning algorithms, robots can tailor meals to individual preferences and dietary needs. By analyzing customer data, these systems can recommend dishes based on past orders, allergies, and nutritional goals. This level of customization enhances the dining experience, making it more enjoyable and satisfying for each customer.

However, the rise of robotic restaurants also raises questions about the future of human interaction in dining. Traditionally, dining out has been a social activity that involves interaction with servers, chefs, and fellow diners. The shift towards automation may reduce these human connections, potentially leading to a more isolated and impersonal dining experience. It is essential to strike a balance between efficiency and human touch, ensuring that technology enhances rather than diminishes the social aspects of dining.

Looking ahead, the future of dining is likely to be a hybrid of robotic and human elements. While automation can streamline processes and improve efficiency, the human touch remains essential in creating memorable and meaningful dining experiences. By integrating robotics into the culinary world thoughtfully and ethically, we can create a future where technology and tradition coexist harmoniously.

6

Chapter 7: The Role of AI in Culinary Innovation

rtificial intelligence (AI) plays a crucial role in driving culinary innovation by providing chefs with powerful tools to experiment and create new dishes. AI algorithms can analyze vast amounts of data, including recipes, ingredient combinations, and cooking techniques, to generate new ideas and insights. This data-driven approach allows chefs to explore novel flavor pairings, develop unique recipes, and refine their culinary techniques.

One of the most exciting applications of AI in culinary innovation is the use of machine learning to predict flavor profiles. By analyzing the chemical composition of ingredients and their interactions, AI can suggest flavor combinations that are both surprising and harmonious. This capability enables chefs to push the boundaries of traditional cuisine and create dishes that challenge and delight the palate.

In addition to flavor prediction, AI can also assist in optimizing cooking processes. By analyzing factors such as temperature, cooking time, and ingredient proportions, AI algorithms can identify the optimal conditions for preparing specific dishes. This level of precision ensures that each dish is cooked to perfection, enhancing both the taste and texture of the food. Furthermore, AI can help chefs experiment with new cooking techniques, such as sous-vide or molecular gastronomy, by providing data-driven insights and recommendations.

AI also has the potential to revolutionize menu development and customization. By analyzing customer preferences and feedback, AI can identify trends and suggest new menu items that cater to evolving tastes and dietary needs. This capability allows restaurants to stay ahead of culinary trends and continuously innovate to meet customer expectations. Additionally, AI-powered recommendation systems can provide personalized dining experiences by suggesting dishes based on individual preferences and dietary restrictions.

However, the integration of AI into culinary innovation is not without its challenges. One of the primary concerns is the potential loss of human creativity and intuition in the cooking process. While AI can provide valuable insights and suggestions, it lacks the emotional and cultural context that human chefs bring to their craft. It is essential to strike a balance between leveraging AI for its analytical capabilities and preserving the artistry and intuition that define exceptional cuisine.

Ultimately, the role of AI in culinary innovation is to complement and enhance the creative process. By providing chefs with data-driven insights and tools, AI can inspire new ideas and enable culinary experimentation. This collaborative approach ensures that the future of food is both innovative and deeply rooted in human creativity and tradition.

Chapter 8: The Impact of Culinary Robotics on Food Sustainability

The integration of culinary robotics into the food industry has significant implications for sustainability and environmental impact. As the global population continues to grow, the demand for food is increasing, placing strain on natural resources and ecosystems. Culinary robotics offers potential solutions to these challenges by improving efficiency, reducing waste, and promoting sustainable practices in food production and consumption.

One of the key benefits of culinary robotics is the ability to optimize resource use in food preparation. Robots can precisely measure and control ingredients, minimizing waste and ensuring that each dish is prepared with the exact amount of resources needed. This level of precision helps reduce food waste, which is a major contributor to environmental degradation. By minimizing waste, culinary robotics contributes to a more sustainable and efficient food supply chain.

In addition to reducing waste, culinary robotics can also enhance energy efficiency in food production. Advanced robotic systems can optimize cooking processes to minimize energy consumption, reducing the carbon footprint of food preparation. For example, robots can use sensors and algorithms to adjust cooking temperatures and times, ensuring that energy is used efficiently. This not only reduces environmental impact but also lowers operational costs for restaurants and food producers.

Moreover, the use of robotics in food production can promote sustainable sourcing and supply chain practices. By integrating AI and data analytics, robots can track and manage inventory, ensuring that ingredients are sourced sustainably and used efficiently. This capability allows for better management of food supply chains, reducing the environmental impact of transportation and storage. Additionally, robotics can support the development of innovative sustainable practices, such as vertical farming and plant-based proteins, by providing the precision and control needed for these emerging technologies.

However, the integration of culinary robotics into the food industry also raises ethical and environmental considerations. The production and disposal of robotic equipment have their own environmental impact, and it is essential to develop sustainable practices for managing the lifecycle of these technologies. Additionally, ensuring that the benefits of culinary robotics are accessible to all, regardless of socio-economic status, is crucial for promoting equitable and sustainable food systems.

By addressing these challenges thoughtfully and collaboratively, we can harness the potential of culinary robotics to promote sustainability and reduce the environmental impact of food production. This approach ensures that the future of food is not only innovative and efficient but also environmentally responsible and socially equitable.

8

Chapter 9: The Intersection of Culinary Arts and Technology

The fusion of culinary arts and technology has transformed the way we approach food preparation, consumption, and experience. This intersection has created new opportunities for innovation and creativity, allowing chefs to explore new techniques, flavors, and presentations. By integrating advanced technologies such as robotics, AI, and data analytics, the culinary world is evolving into a dynamic and exciting field that pushes the boundaries of traditional cuisine.

One of the most significant impacts of technology on the culinary arts is the ability to experiment with new cooking techniques. Innovations such as sous-vide, molecular gastronomy, and 3D food printing have expanded the possibilities for chefs, allowing them to create dishes that are visually stunning and texturally unique. These techniques require precision and control, which can be achieved through the use of advanced robotics and AI. By leveraging these technologies, chefs can push the limits of their creativity and create culinary masterpieces that captivate and delight diners.

In addition to new cooking techniques, technology has also transformed the way we experience food. Virtual reality (VR) and augmented reality (AR) are being used to create immersive dining experiences that engage multiple senses. For example, diners can wear VR headsets to be transported to a different environment while enjoying their meal, enhancing the overall sensory experience. AR can be used to provide interactive menus and visualizations of dishes, allowing diners to explore and customize their meals before ordering. These technologies add a new dimension to the dining experience, making it more interactive and engaging.

Furthermore, the integration of technology into the culinary world has opened up new possibilities for collaboration and knowledge sharing. Online platforms and social media have created a global community of chefs and food enthusiasts who can share their ideas, techniques, and recipes. This collaborative approach fosters innovation and allows for the rapid dissemination of culinary knowledge. Additionally, AI-powered tools can analyze and categorize vast amounts of culinary data, making it easier for chefs to access and learn from the experiences of others.

However, the intersection of culinary arts and technology also raises questions about the preservation of traditional techniques and cultural heritage. While technology enables new forms of culinary expression, it is essential to balance innovation with the preservation of culinary traditions. By honoring the past while embracing the future, we can ensure that the culinary arts continue to evolve in a way that respects and celebrates cultural diversity.

Ultimately, the fusion of culinary arts and technology represents a harmonious blend of creativity, precision, and innovation. By leveraging the strengths of both human ingenuity and technological advancements, we can create a future where food is not only a source of sustenance but also a medium for artistic expression and cultural exploration.

9

Chapter 10: The Role of Robotics in Global Food Security

The integration of robotics into the food industry has the potential to address some of the most pressing challenges related to global food security. As the world population continues to grow, ensuring access to safe, nutritious, and affordable food for all is a critical priority. Culinary robotics offers innovative solutions to improve food production, distribution, and accessibility, contributing to a more resilient and equitable global food system.

One of the key ways in which robotics can enhance global food security is by increasing the efficiency and productivity of food production. Automated systems can optimize farming practices, such as planting, harvesting, and irrigation, to maximize crop yields and reduce resource use. Additionally, robotics can support precision agriculture, where sensors and algorithms are used to monitor and manage crops with high accuracy. This approach minimizes minimizes resource wastage and maximizes the potential of agricultural land.

In the realm of food distribution, robotics can streamline the supply chain, reducing delays and losses associated with manual handling. Automated warehouses and robotic delivery systems ensure that food is transported and stored under optimal conditions, maintaining its quality and safety. This enhanced efficiency in the supply chain can reduce food spoilage and waste, ensuring that more food reaches those in need.

Moreover, robotics can play a crucial role in improving accessibility to nutritious food in underserved communities. Automated systems can assist in the production of affordable and nutrient-dense food products, such as plant-based proteins and fortified staples. By reducing production costs and improving efficiency, culinary robotics can make healthy food options more accessible and affordable for all, addressing issues of malnutrition and food insecurity.

However, the integration of robotics into the global food system also raises ethical and social considerations. Ensuring that the benefits of these technologies are equitably distributed is essential to avoid exacerbating existing disparities. Additionally, it is crucial to develop policies and regulations that support sustainable and responsible use of robotics in food production and distribution.

By leveraging the potential of culinary robotics, we can work towards a future where food security is ensured for all, and the global food system is resilient, efficient, and sustainable. This collaborative effort requires the involvement of policymakers, technologists, farmers, and communities to create a just and equitable food system for all.

10

Chapter 11: The Cultural Impact of Culinary Robotics

The fusion of culinary robotics and cultural traditions presents a fascinating interplay between innovation and heritage. As robots become more integrated into the culinary world, they influence and are influenced by diverse cultural practices and cuisines. This cultural exchange has the potential to enrich the culinary landscape, fostering creativity and cross-cultural understanding.

One of the ways in which culinary robotics interacts with culture is through the preservation and dissemination of traditional recipes. Robots can be programmed to replicate age-old cooking techniques and recipes with precision, ensuring that these culinary traditions are preserved for future generations. This capability is particularly valuable in regions where traditional knowledge is at risk of being lost due to modernization and globalization. By documenting and automating these recipes, we can celebrate and safeguard cultural heritage.

Culinary robotics also facilitates the fusion of different culinary traditions, leading to the creation of innovative and diverse dishes. By leveraging advanced technology, chefs can experiment with blending flavors and techniques from various cultures, resulting in unique culinary experiences. This fusion not only expands the culinary repertoire but also promotes cultural exchange and appreciation, breaking down barriers and fostering connections between people from different backgrounds.

However, the integration of robotics into the culinary world also raises questions about cultural appropriation and authenticity. It is essential to approach the use of technology in cooking with respect and sensitivity to the cultural significance of traditional practices. By engaging with communities and honoring the origins of culinary traditions, we can ensure that innovation is carried out in a way that respects and celebrates cultural diversity.

The cultural impact of culinary robotics extends beyond the kitchen to the way we experience and appreciate food. As robots become more involved in the culinary arts, they challenge our perceptions of creativity, artistry, and the human touch in cooking. This evolving relationship between technology and culture invites us to reflect on the ways in which we define and value culinary traditions and innovations.

Ultimately, the fusion of culinary robotics and cultural traditions offers an opportunity to create a richer and more diverse culinary landscape. By embracing both innovation and heritage, we can celebrate the unique flavors and techniques that define different cultures while exploring new possibilities for culinary creativity.

11

Chapter 12: The Future of Culinary Robotics: Possibilities and Challenges

The future of culinary robotics is full of exciting possibilities and challenges as technology continues to advance and become more integrated into our daily lives. As we look ahead, several trends and innovations are likely to shape the future of the culinary world, transforming the way we prepare, consume, and experience food.

One of the most promising trends is the development of increasingly sophisticated robotic systems that can perform a wider range of culinary tasks. Advances in artificial intelligence, machine learning, and robotics will enable machines to handle more complex and intricate cooking techniques, from pastry arts to fine dining. These advancements will allow chefs to push the boundaries of their creativity, exploring new culinary horizons and elevating the dining experience.

Another key area of innovation is the use of robotics in personalized nutrition and health. As our understanding of nutrition and its impact on health grows, robots will play a crucial role in creating customized meals tailored to individual dietary needs and preferences. By analyzing data on nutrition, health conditions, and personal preferences, robots can design and prepare meals that support optimal health and well-being. This personalized approach to nutrition has the potential to revolutionize the way we approach food and health, making it easier for individuals to achieve their dietary goals.

The future of culinary robotics also holds the potential for more sustainable and environmentally friendly food practices. Innovations in precision agriculture, vertical farming, and lab-grown foods will reduce the environmental impact of food production and promote more sustainable practices. Robots will play a crucial role in optimizing these processes, ensuring efficient use of resources and minimizing waste. By embracing these technologies, we can work towards a more sustainable and resilient global food system.

However, the future of culinary robotics also presents several challenges that must be addressed. Ensuring equitable access to advanced technologies is essential to avoid exacerbating existing disparities in food security and nutrition. Additionally, the ethical considerations of job displacement, data privacy, and cultural preservation must be carefully navigated to ensure that the integration of robotics into the culinary world is carried out responsibly and thoughtfully.

As we move forward, it is essential to foster collaboration between technologists, chefs, policymakers, and communities to create a future where culinary robotics enhances and enriches our culinary experiences. By embracing innovation while honoring tradition, we can build a culinary landscape that is both dynamic and inclusive, celebrating the diversity of flavors and cultures that define our shared human experience.

12

Chapter 13: The Evolution of Culinary Robotics Technology

As we journey deeper into the future of culinary robotics, it's essential to explore the evolution of this technology and how it has shaped the modern culinary landscape. The development of culinary robotics has been marked by significant advancements in artificial intelligence, machine learning, and robotics engineering. These technologies have enabled robots to perform increasingly complex tasks, from precise measurements and cooking techniques to intricate plating and presentation.

One of the key milestones in the evolution of culinary robotics is the introduction of advanced sensory systems. Equipped with high-resolution cameras, pressure sensors, and temperature controls, modern culinary robots can replicate the sensory experience of human chefs. These sensory systems allow robots to adjust cooking times, temperatures, and ingredient proportions based on real-time feedback, ensuring that each dish is prepared to perfection.

Another important advancement is the development of collaborative robots, or cobots, which are designed to work alongside human chefs in the kitchen. Cobots are equipped with safety features and intuitive interfaces that enable them to assist with repetitive or labor-intensive tasks while allowing human chefs to focus on creative and innovative aspects of cooking.

This collaboration between humans and robots enhances efficiency and productivity in professional kitchens, leading to higher-quality dishes and more enjoyable dining experiences.

The integration of AI and machine learning has also played a crucial role in the evolution of culinary robotics. AI algorithms can analyze vast amounts of culinary data, including recipes, ingredient interactions, and cooking techniques, to generate new insights and ideas. Machine learning enables robots to learn from their experiences and improve their performance over time, making them more adaptable and capable of handling complex culinary tasks. This continuous improvement ensures that culinary robotics will continue to evolve and push the boundaries of culinary innovation.

Looking ahead, the future of culinary robotics technology holds even more exciting possibilities. Advances in quantum computing, bioengineering, and nanotechnology may lead to the development of even more sophisticated and versatile culinary robots. These future technologies will enable robots to perform tasks that are currently beyond their capabilities, further transforming the culinary landscape and redefining the art of cooking.

13

Chapter 14: Culinary Robotics in Space Exploration

The application of culinary robotics extends beyond Earth, playing a crucial role in the future of space exploration and long-duration space missions. As humanity embarks on journeys to Mars and beyond, ensuring access to nutritious and enjoyable food is essential for the well-being and morale of astronauts. Culinary robotics offers innovative solutions to address the unique challenges of space food preparation, storage, and consumption.

One of the primary challenges of space food is the limited availability of fresh ingredients. Culinary robots can assist in the cultivation of fresh produce in space, using advanced hydroponic and aeroponic systems to grow fruits and vegetables in controlled environments. These robotic systems can monitor and adjust growth conditions, ensuring optimal yields and nutrient content. This capability allows astronauts to enjoy fresh and nutritious food, reducing reliance on pre-packaged meals and enhancing their overall health and well-being.

In addition to growing fresh produce, culinary robots can also assist in preparing and cooking meals in microgravity environments. Traditional cooking methods are often impractical in space due to the absence of gravity, which can cause ingredients and liquids to float away. Culinary robots can be designed to handle these challenges, using secure enclosures and advanced cooking techniques to prepare meals in a controlled and efficient manner. This ensures that astronauts can enjoy a variety of delicious and comforting meals, even in the harsh conditions of space.

Culinary robotics also plays a role in addressing the psychological and social aspects of space food. The act of sharing meals and enjoying familiar flavors can provide a sense of comfort and normalcy for astronauts, helping to alleviate feelings of isolation and stress. Robotic systems can be programmed to recreate favorite recipes and dishes, allowing astronauts to experience the tastes of home while far away from Earth. This connection to familiar foods can have a positive impact on mental health and overall well-being during long-duration space missions.

As space exploration continues to advance, culinary robotics will play an increasingly important role in ensuring that astronauts have access to nutritious, enjoyable, and culturally significant food. By leveraging the capabilities of robotics, we can support the physical and psychological needs of astronauts, enabling them to thrive in the challenging environments of space.

14

Chapter 15: The Philosophy of Culinary Robotics

The fusion of culinary arts and robotics invites us to explore the philosophical implications of this technological evolution. As we integrate robots into the culinary world, we are confronted with questions about creativity, authenticity, and the essence of the human experience in cooking. These philosophical considerations challenge us to reflect on the nature of culinary artistry and the role of technology in shaping our relationship with food.

One of the central philosophical questions is the nature of creativity in cooking. While robots can replicate recipes with precision and consistency, they lack the intuition, spontaneity, and emotional depth that characterize human creativity. The act of cooking is often seen as an expression of personal and cultural identity, where chefs infuse their dishes with their unique experiences, memories, and emotions. As we integrate robotics into the culinary arts, we must consider how to preserve and celebrate this human element of creativity, ensuring that technology enhances rather than diminishes the artistry of cooking.

Authenticity is another important philosophical consideration in the age of culinary robotics. The rise of automation raises questions about the authenticity of robotically prepared dishes and their connection to traditional culinary practices. While robots can replicate the techniques and ingredients of traditional recipes, they lack the cultural and historical context that human chefs bring to their craft. It is essential to balance the efficiency and innovation offered by robotics with a deep respect for the cultural significance and authenticity of culinary traditions.

The integration of robotics into the culinary world also invites us to reflect on the essence of the human experience in cooking and eating. Food is not only a source of sustenance but also a medium for social connection, cultural expression, and personal enjoyment. As robots take on more tasks in the kitchen, we must consider how to maintain the human touch and the social and emotional aspects of cooking and dining. This includes finding ways to incorporate technology that enhances the dining experience while preserving the rituals and traditions that make food a meaningful part of our lives.

Ultimately, the philosophy of culinary robotics challenges us to consider the broader implications of integrating technology into the culinary arts. By engaging with these philosophical questions, we can navigate the evolving landscape of food and technology with thoughtfulness and intention, ensuring that the future of culinary robotics is guided by principles of creativity, authenticity, and human connection.

Book Description: Culinary Code: The Fusion of Robotics, Sociology, and the Art of Eating

Dive into a groundbreaking exploration of the culinary world where robotics, sociology, and the art of eating converge in "Culinary Code." This captivating book takes readers on a journey through the intersection of advanced technology and timeless culinary traditions, revealing how robots are transforming the way we prepare, consume, and experience food.

From the precision and efficiency of culinary robots in professional kitchens to the ethical implications of automation in the food industry, "Culinary Code" delves into the multifaceted impact of robotics on our eating habits and social dynamics. Discover how AI and machine learning are driving culinary innovation, creating personalized dining experiences, and even supporting global food security.

Through engaging chapters, readers will explore the evolution of culinary robotics technology, the integration of robots into space exploration, and the philosophical questions surrounding creativity and authenticity in cooking. The book also highlights the cultural significance of food, examining how culinary robotics can preserve and celebrate diverse culinary traditions while fostering cross-cultural connections.

"Culinary Code" offers a thought-provoking and comprehensive look at the future of food, where technology and tradition blend seamlessly to create a richer and more dynamic culinary landscape. Whether you're a food enthusiast, a tech aficionado, or simply curious about the future of dining, this book provides a unique and insightful perspective on the fusion of robotics and the culinary arts.